The World of Nature

Exploring nature
with hands-on learning activities

by
Wendy Pfeffer

Art by
Susan Krackehl

FIRST TEACHER PRESS
First Teacher Press,Inc./Bridgeport,CT

For Tim, who has already discovered the wonderful world of nature,
and
For Tom, who is always there for me.
With special thanks to Lisa Durkin for her expert guidance.

ISBN   1-878727-03-6

Cover and Page Design: Gene Krackehl
Cover photo: Andrew Brilliant and Carol Palmer (taken at Westfield Child Center, Brockton, MA)

Edited by Margery Kranyik, Mary Lee Johansen
Editorial Assistants: Jessica Rubenstein, Alicia La-France, Thomas Jenen
Skills Chart: Martha A. Hayes
Art Editor: Debby Dixler
Spot Art: Nina Gaelen
Computer Graphics: Jill Levine
Typesetting and Layout: Anita Golton, Jeffrey Goldfarb
Manufactured in the United States of America

Special thanks to Lisa Schustak, Jennifer Durkin, and Janet Schuman.

Published by First Teacher Press, First Teacher, Inc.
P.O. Box 29, 60 Main Street, Bridgeport, CT 06602

TABLE OF CONTENTS

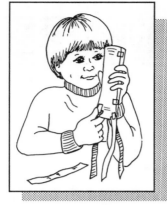

INTRODUCTION

The creative activities in *The World of Nature* are designed to help children discover concepts in nature and to foster the development of important basic skills. Children learn to follow directions, make observations, classify, recognize or show sequence, group, label, record, and compare through projects, games, and experiments that are both fun and challenging to the young learner. Fine motor dexterity is promoted through tracing, drawing, cutting, and gluing.

These hands-on activities are planned so that children will build a store of general knowledge while learning about the world of nature. Crafts, creative movement activities, books, recipes, and experiments help children better understand concepts and to realize more clearly the connections between the activities and other events in their world.

To help you fit them into your existing curriculum, the activities in *The World of Nature* are divided into five major categories:

• Plants
• Animals
• Weather
• Earth, Seas, and Sky
• Experiments

Projects, experiments, and games in *The World of Nature* encourage children to explore the environment through their senses in order to develop an interest in weather, animals, plants, insects, and the world around them. The activities can be tailored easily for children of different age and developmental levels. They can be used with both individuals and small groups.

As with most activities for young children, what children experience as they do the activity is much more important than the final product. You know the children you teach and will want to adapt the activities in this book to your teaching style and to meet the individual needs in your group. With some children, you may have to do one or more steps, such as folding a paper or writing a word. Here are some other adaptations you may want to consider. If some children take longer to color, perhaps they should cut and glue first and leave the coloring to the last. If other children use so much glue that it's impossible for them to crayon over the glue, they should crayon first, then cut and glue.

The goal in *The World of Nature* is to introduce young children to various concepts and facts that they will encounter later in school. These activities are meant to be fun and stimulating—to encourage children to explore nature on their own with a sense of joy and wonder.

Safety Precautions:

Careful supervision is necessary for each activity included in this book, but especially the cooking projects and experiments. Also only non-toxic supplies, crayons, markers, glue, paints, and so on, should be used. Children should be taught to wash their hands after using the materials in each lesson and never to put anything but food in their mouths.

In *The World of Nature*, following each re-producible activity sheet there is a complete lesson plan. Each Lesson Plan is divided into six easy-to-use sections.

Objectives:

This section lets you know some of the child-centered goals for each activity. All of the activities stimulate creativity, develop fine motor skills, reinforce following directions, and promote cooperation and social interaction. Complete mastery of a skill or understanding of a concept is never the goal of any activity. We recognize that many, many experiences, coupled with developmental maturation, are necessary for a child's complete mastery or understanding of information given or skill presented. The activities in *The World of Nature* will provide some of these valuable experiences.

What You'll Need:

Here we tell you what you'll need to have on hand to help children complete each basic activity with ease. For each activity, we provide you with a quick, "no-frills" supply list. The supplies are inexpensive materials that are either common to most early childhood classrooms or throw-aways from home.

Introduction:

In this section, we offer you some creative ideas for introducing and discussing the topic which is the focus of each activity. In addition, because we know that children arrive at your door each day packed with information and experiences of their own, we suggest ways for their own prior knowledge as springboards for further exploration.

What to Do:

Here you'll get specific, step-by-step instructions to help you guide children as they complete each basic activity. At a glance you'll be able to see the most basic application for each activity page. The activities are open-ended enough to provide for much creativity and for different levels of development.

Challenge:

Through the project(s) in the Challenge section children have the opportunity to apply their knowledge of skills and concepts in new and more complicated ways and derive an even greater amount of learning. The Challenge section will help you individualize the use of each Activity Sheet to meet various needs of your children.

Making Connections:

For children's learning to be meaningful, they must connect what they are learning with what they already know, in the form of "real-life" projects. "Making Connections" offers you a wealth of ideas for relating the information and concepts from each activity to other areas of children's curriculum, and thus to real life.

Books to Read:

At the end of each lesson plan, one or more books are suggested to enhance the topic of the lesson. These books can be read and discussed at circletime or placed in the reading area for individual exploration by children.

Skills Chart

Act. #	Activity Name	Noting Cause and Effect	Classifying	Making Comparisons	Demonstrating Creative Movement	Noting Details	Following Directions	Drawing Inferences	Labeling	Developing Listening Skills	Matching	Making Observations	Predicting Outcomes	Keeping Records	Showing Sequence	Working with Math Concepts
1.	Adopt a Tree			•		•										•
2.	Leaf Rubbings		•	•		•					•					•
3.	Growing Bulbs														•	
4.	Vegetable Soup		•			•			•							
5.	Pets and Zoo Animals		•			•		•	•							
6.	Crawlers and Jumpers		•		•				•							
7.	Farm Families		•	•					•		•					
8.	Caterpillars and Butterflies						•			•					•	
9.	Weather Chart		•			•		•						•		
10.	Wind Sock						•	•							•	
11.	Rainbows	•				•										
12.	The Four Seasons		•												•	
13.	Make a Volcano											•		•	•	
14.	Rock Collection		•	•		•									•	
15.	Summer Fun		•													
16.	A Home for the Fish		•					•								
17.	Things in the Sky		•					•								
18.	Sink and Float		•			•							•	•		
19.	Magnet Fun		•			•						•		•		
20.	Absorption		•			•						•		•		
21.	Hot or Cold		•			•						•		•		

ADOPT A TREE

OBJECTIVES:
- to note details (about trees);
- to practice using nonstandard measurement.

This activity is good to start at the beginning of the school year. Continue observation of each child's tree throughout the four seasons.

What You'll Need:
Copies of Activity 1 • crayons or markers • scissors • yarn • glue.

Introduction:
Explore the trees around your school—in the play yard, the park, and the surrounding area. Talk about the similarities and differences. Play games with children: Ask: *"Who can find the thickest tree trunk? Let's see how many different kinds of leaves we can find."* Look at trees in books on nature and notice and compare illustrations of trees in story books.

What to Do:
1. Tell children that they are each going to adopt a tree. (Every child may adopt the same tree if they need to.) Once they have decided on the tree they wish to adopt, give out copies of Activity 1. Explain that children are going to record information about their tree on the Activity Sheet.

2. Have children draw a picture of their tree in the frame at the top of the Sheet. If possible, let them actually view the tree as they draw it.
3. Have children visit their tree and find a piece of bark to paste in the square on the sheet. If no bark pieces can be found, show children how to put their sheet up against the trunk and make a rubbing of the bark with a crayon in the square.
4. Help each child measure the trunk of his tree with a piece of yarn. Have children glue their yarn at the bottom of the Sheet.
5. Finally, have each child find a leaf from his tree and glue the leaf onto the Sheet in the rectangle shape.

Challenge:
- Make additional copies of the Activity Sheet and have children fill it in at different seasons of the year. Discuss the changes which occur.

Making Connections:
- Have children measure other objects with yarn and compare these measurements with their tree trunk. (Math)
- Have each child name his tree and dictate and illustrate a story about it. Children might wish to write about the animals or insects which live in their tree. (Language)

Book to Read:
The Giving Tree by Shel Silverstein (Harper and Row)

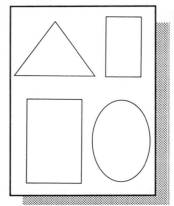

LEAF RUBBINGS

OBJECTIVES:
- to recognize and identify different shapes (in leaves);
- to compare and match items (leaves);
- to classify (according to color, size).

This fall activity combines concepts and skills related to science, math, and art.

What You'll Need:
Copies of Activity 2 • paper bags • red, yellow, brown, and orange crayons.

Introduction:
Give each child a paper bag and go for a walk in a park or wooded area. Help children collect fallen leaves of different sizes, shapes, and colors. Sit together near a pile of leaves and have children close their eyes and talk about the sounds and smells they experience.

What to Do:
1. Provide each child with a copy of Activity 2. Help children identify the shapes.
2. Have children look through the leaves they have collected outside and select a leaf that is similar in size and shape to each of the shapes on the Activity Sheet. Encourage children to experiment by placing various leaves on the shapes before deciding on the best matches.
3. Demonstrate how the leaf can be placed on a hard, flat surface, then the Activity Sheet placed over it, with the correct shape on top of the leaf. Show how your fingers can feel the position of the leaf under the sheet.
4. Help children place one leaf (vein side up) under the matching shape on their sheet. Provide crayons and have children choose one crayon and, holding it

on an angle, rub the crayon on the sheet so that the leaf shape and veins appear as lines within or near the outlined shape. Have children make rubbings with other leaves within the other shapes.

Challenges:
- Have children sort the leaves they collected by shape. Then have them re-sort the leaves by color and then by size.
- Help children choose three or four leaves of the same color or shape. Have each child put her group of leaves in order from smallest to largest.

Making Connections:
- Make leaf skeletons by mixing equal amounts of white sugar, bleach, and detergent in an aluminum pan. Add a leaf to the pan and boil on top of the stove for about twelve minutes. When cool, remove the leaf carefully and spray with water in the sink until the color between the veins disappears. Rinse and dry flat on a paper towel. (Science)

Book to Read:
Leaves by Fulvio Testa (Peter Bedrick)

GROWING BULBS

OBJECTIVES:
- to recognize and show sequence (of a task).

This is a good activity to do in the spring.

What You'll Need:
Copies of Activity 3 • scissors • glue • crayons or markers • blank pieces of paper • three or four hyacinth or narcissus bulbs • a shallow dish • pebbles.

Introduction:
Bring in some bulbs to show children. Ask, "What are these?" "What is inside of each one?" (leaves, flower, bud, food) "What might grow from these bulbs?" (Have a picture of the flower that will grow from the bulb.) Follow these directions to help children plant the bulbs.
1. Put an inch of pebbles in the dish.
2. Put bulbs close together in the dish with the roots (flat side) down.
3. Put more pebbles in the dish. Leave the top half of each bulb showing.
4. Add water to the top of the pebbles. Keep them wet.
5. Place the dish in a cool, sunny spot for five weeks. Watch the bulbs grow.

What to Do:
1. Provide each child with a copy of Activity 3 and discuss the pictures. Have scissors, paper and glue available.
2. Have children cut out the four pictures and glue them in order on a blank piece of paper to show how the bulbs were planted. Help children write their names on their papers and collect them.
3. In two or three weeks, pull one bulb up. Have children note the roots. Pass out each child's paper. Have crayons or markers available. Have children add roots to the bulbs in the final picture in the sequence. Then collect the papers again.
4. When the bulbs bloom, pass out children's papers. Once again, make crayons or markers available. Have children add the newest changes to the bulbs in the final picture.

Challenge:
- Have children tell what happened to the bulbs from planting to blooming, using their papers as a guide.

Making Connections:
- Have children glue the shape of a container cut from wallpaper, fabric, or metallic paper at the bottom of a piece of blank paper. Help children roll small pieces of colored paper, one inch by three inches, around a pencil. Then have children glue the paper curl just above the container with the curl facing down. The three dimensional effect of the finished picture looks just like a hyacinth. (Art)

- Describe the growing process while children use their whole bodies to act out the growth of a bulb. (Creative Movement)

Book to Read:
Bulbs, Corn ,and Such by Millicent Selsam (Morrow)

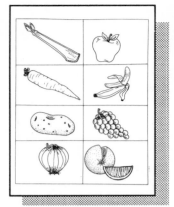

VEGETABLE SOUP

OBJECTIVES:
- to recognize and identify specific vegetables and fruits;
- to classify and label (foods);
- to use senses (smell, taste) to identify foods.

Children will learn about vegetables and fruits through all of their senses as they help prepare a simple recipe.

What You'll Need:
Copies of Activity 4 • scissors • glue • blank pieces of paper • crayons or markers • plastic knives • large pot • RECIPE INGREDIENTS: celery • carrots • potato • onion • bouillon cubes • measuring cup • water.

Introduction:
Read a version of the folk tale "Stone Soup." Display the vegetables listed above. Help children identify them. Rinse vegetables and peel the potato and onion. Then let children smell and taste each one. Help children cut up the vegetables with plastic knives, put them in a large pot, add enough water to cover the vegetables, and add bouillon cubes (one cube for each cup of water). Bring to a boil and then simmer for about one hour to make vegetable soup.

What to Do:
1. Provide each child with a copy of Activity 4. Have crayons or markers, blank pieces of paper, scissors, and glue available for use by small groups.
2. Help children identify on the Activity Sheet the vegetables they used to make the soup. Then have children color in the vegetables. If possible, keep extra vegetables from the soup recipe on hand for reference.
3. Give each child a piece of paper. Help children draw or trace a big circle (soup pot) on the paper. (Circles may need to be pre-drawn for younger children.)
4. Have children cut out the vegetables and glue them in the circle (pot).

Challenge:
- Have children look at the remaining pictures and decide what group they belong to (fruits). Bring in an orange, apple, banana, and grapes. Let children smell and taste each one. Then help children cut up the fruits with plastic knives to make fruit salad.

Making Connections:
- Have pictures of the five categories of food each of us should have every day: grains, protein, dairy, fruits, and vegetables. Ask children to name examples of a food in each category. Have children cut out and glue a picture of food from each category on a paper plate, to take home to share with their families. (Science)

Books to Read:
Growing Vegetable Soup by Lois Ehlert (Harcourt)
Stone Soup by Marcia Brown (Macmillan)

PETS AND WILD ANIMALS

OBJECTIVES:
- to recognize and identify specific animals;
- to discover appropriate environments for specific animals;
- to classify (animals, environments).

Children enjoy studying about animals. This activity explores the animal world to help children discover where animals live.

What You'll Need:
Copies of Activity 5 • crayons or markers • blank pieces of paper • scissors • glue.

Introduction:
Ask children: *"How many of you have a pet at home?"* After children have discussed their pets, ask: *"Do any of you have a camel at home?"* Discuss reasons for not having some animals as pets and why some animals live in the wild or in a zoo. Encourage children to talk about their personal zoo experiences.

What to Do:
1. Provide each child with a copy of Activity 5 and scissors. Have blank paper, glue, and markers available.
2. Help children identify the animals on the Activity Sheet.
3. Have children cut out the animals and group them according to whether or not they would make good house pets. Discuss children's groupings.
4. Give children pieces of blank paper. Have them choose one animal that they would like to have as a pet and glue it on the paper.
5. Have each child draw accessories for the pet they chose on the paper (a bed, some toys, and food for their pet).

Challenges:
- Have children choose another animal, this time one that would be better off living in the wild or in a zoo environment. Have them glue this animal onto a blank sheet of paper and create an environment for it.
- Help children verbally reclassify the animals in both groups by type: animals that live on land, animals that live in water, and animals that fly.

Making Connections:
- Have children choose an animal and move like that animal. See if others can identify the animal. (Creative Movement)

- Play sections of music from *Carnival of Animals* by Camille Saint-Saens, and "Daddy's Taking Me to the Zoo Tomorrow" by Peter, Paul and Mary on *Peter, Paul and Mommy* recording. (Music)

Books to Read:
Annie and the Wild Animals by Jan Brett (Houghton Mifflin)
These are My Pets by Mercer Mayer (Golden)

CRAWLERS AND JUMPERS

OBJECTIVES:
- to recognize and identify certain specific animals;
- to classify (according to motion);
- to explore concepts through creative movement.

Children can relate to members of the animal kingdom through creative movement experiences that pantomime how certain animals move.

What You'll Need:
Copies of Activity 6 • scissors • glue • crayons or markers • blank pieces of paper.

Introduction:
Ask children what animals they can think of that crawl, jump, or hop. Then play peppy music and have children jump around the room imitating animal jumpers. Suggest that they jump on two feet and then on one foot (hop). Then play slow, smooth music and have children get on all fours and crawl like a baby. Vary the music and have children listen for and react to the changes. Have children tell what animals they are imitating as they move.

What to Do:
1. Provide each child with a copy of Activity 6. Have crayons or markers, scissors, glue, and pieces of paper available.
2. Help children identify the animals and insects on the Activity Sheet. Then have them take turns acting out how these animals move.
3. Have children color and cut out the pictures. Give children pieces of paper and have them glue the crawlers onto the bottom of the paper and the jumpers onto the top of the paper.

Challenge:
- Make more copies of the Activity Sheet. Back them with cardboard and let children color the animals. Then cut out the individual pictures. Place pictures in a pile face down and have children take turns picking a card and acting out the movements of that creature. Add pictures of other animals that have distinctive ways of moving (for example, fish, bear, elephant, bird, etc.). After a while, let children add sounds to their imitations.

Making Connections:
- Help children use clay or play dough to make creatures which crawl or jump. (Art)
- Sing this song to the tune of "Here we go 'round the mulberry bush." Add appropriate movements.

> *This is the way we jump like crickets,*
> *Jump like crickets, jump like crickets,*
> *This is the way we jump like crickets,*
> *All around the meadow.*
> *This is the way we hop like rabbits...*
> *This is the way we crawl like snakes...*
> *This is the way we wriggle like*
> *worms...*
>
> (Music, Creative Movement)

Books to Read:
Hop, Skip, Jump-a-roo Zoo by Jane Monecure (Child's World)
National Worm Day by James Stevenson (Greenwillow)

FARM FAMILIES

OBJECTIVES:

- to introduce concept of a farm environment;
- to recognize and identify specific farm animals;
- to match (children and young animals with their parents).

We look to the farm for many of the things we eat and use. Introduce children to the concept and make-up of a farm and the plants and animals which provide much of the fresh produce and dairy products they eat.

What You'll Need:

Copies of Activity 7 • crayons or markers • cloth • mixed media (grass shoots, bits of cotton or wool, straw, feathers) • scissors • glue.

Introduction:

Show children a container of milk. Ask questions such as, *"Where does this milk come from?"* If children answer, *"the store,"* follow up with, *"Where does milk come from before it gets to the store?"* Talk about cows giving us milk and cows living on a farm. Ask if any children have ever been to or lived on a farm. Ask children, *"Do you know of any animals other than cows that live on a farm? How do those animals help us?"*

What to Do:

1. Provide each child with a copy of Activity 7. Have scissors, glue, and crayons or markers available.
2. Have children look at the farm scene and identify all the animals they can. Introduce them to the names of any animals they do not recognize.
3. Have children look at the pictures at the side of the page. Explain that these are the children of some of the people and animals in the farm scene.

4. Have children cut out the pictures of the child and the young animals and glue them next to the matching parent's picture in the scene.
5. Have children color the scene and if possible, help them add mixed media to give the scene a three dimensional effect. For example, put some glue on the paper and add bits of grass, pieces of cloth for clothes, cotton for sheep, etc.

Challenges:

- Talk about fruits and vegetables grown on a farm. Have children find some examples in their farm scene.
- Have children find pictures in magazines or newspapers of products provided by farm animals. Have them cut out the pictures and make a farm collage.

Making Connections:

- Take a trip to a local farm, if possible, and have children create a story about their trip. (Social Studies, Language)

- Play "Farmer in the Dell" using only farm animals. (Creative Movement, Music)

Book to Read:

Animals on the Farm by Feodor Rojankovsky (Knopf)

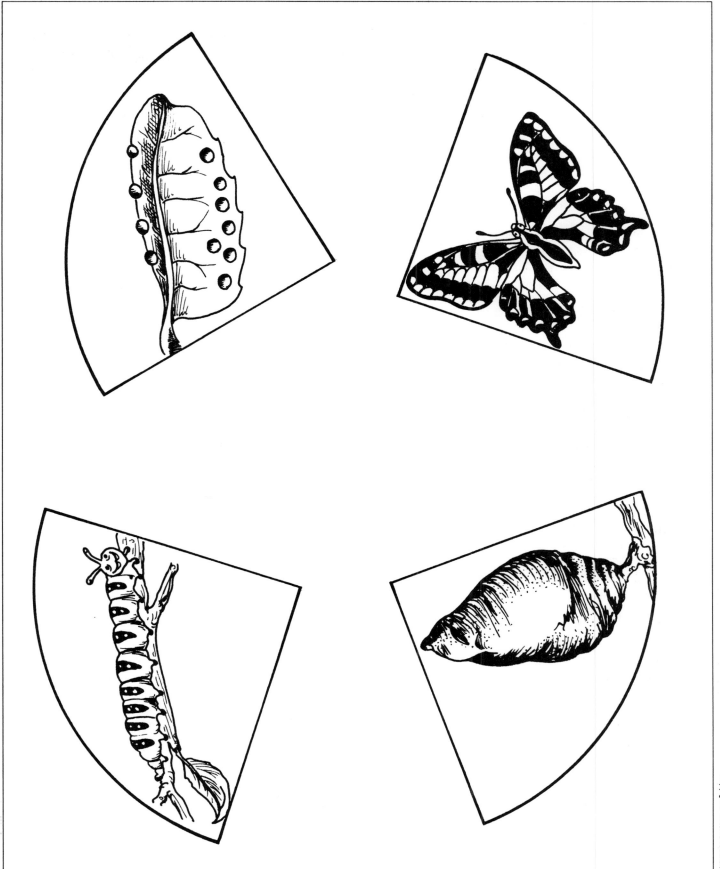

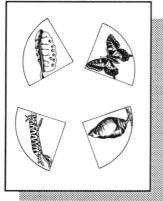

CATERPILLARS AND BUTTERFLIES

OBJECTIVES:
- to show sequence (life cycle);
- to develop listening skills;
- to understand the concept of a life cycle.

This activity will help children understand the sequence of one of the great wonders of nature—the metamorphosis of a caterpillar into a beautiful butterfly.

What You'll Need:
Copies of Activity 8 • scissors • glue • colored markers • six inch paper plates, divided into quarters.

Introduction:
If possible, read *The Very Hungry Caterpillar* by Eric Carle (Philomel) with children. At the end of the story, say: *"And this butterfly laid tiny eggs on a green leaf and a new caterpillar came out..."* Then read the book again. At the end, repeat the sentence above. This repetition helps children understand the concept of the never ending cycle that takes place from egg to caterpillar to cocoon to butterfly and back to egg again. If this book is unavailable, use any book that describes this cycle or use photographs to describe the cycle yourself.

What to Do:
1. Provide each child with a copy of Activity 8 and scissors. Help children identify the pictures; an egg on a leaf, a caterpillar, a cocoon, and a butterfly.
2. Have children color the pictures and then cut them out on the heavy lines.
3. Give each child a six inch paper plate divided with a thick marker into quarters. Help children glue the leaf with the egg in one section of the plate.

4. Now ask children what happens to the egg after a little time. (It hatches into a caterpillar.) Have children glue the caterpillar in the section next to the egg to its right.
5. Repeat with the other stages of development and pictures.

Challenges:
- Give children pieces of cotton and brightly colored tissue paper. Let them glue the cotton on the cocoon and the tissue paper on the wings of the butterfly.

- Have children tell the story of the butterfly using the plate as a guide.

Making Connections:
- Discuss with children the life cycle of a person. People are babies first, then children, then teenagers, then adults. If possible, bring in photographs of yourself at different stages to illustrate the idea. (Science)
- Help children make caterpillars by painting egg cartons split in half and adding pipe cleaners for antennae. (Art)

Books to Read:
Where Does the Butterfly Go When It Rains? by May Garelick (Scott)
From Egg to Butterfly by Marlene Reidel (Carolrhoda)

1

2

3

4

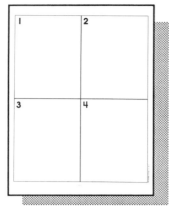

WEATHER CHART

OBJECTIVES:
- to note details and reinforce observation skills;
- to use graphic symbols (to record weather patterns);
- to categorize;
- to make inferences (from graphic symbols).

Changes in weather are caused by the sun which warms the earth and bodies of water causing air to move and rain to fall. Help children observe and record weather patterns where they live.

What You'll Need:
Copies of Activity 9 • scissors • paste • cotton balls • rice • foil or gold circles (stickers) • gray paint.

Introduction:
Play a live or taped weather report or read a report from your local newspaper. Discuss the information with children. Ask questions such as: *"Why is it important for us to know what the weather will be like? Can different types of weather make us feel differently?"* Talk about how our clothing changes according to the weather. Show a weather chart from your local newspaper. Talk about the symbols used to indicate different types of weather. Tell children they are going to keep their own weather chart for a few days, using special symbols. The symbols will show the type of weather: cotton for clouds, gray painted drops for rain, rice for snow, foil or gold circles for sun.

What to Do:
1. Provide each child with Activity 9. Help children put their names on their Activity Sheet. Have glue and art materials available.
2. Each day for four days, have children add one symbol (or more) to the box on their Sheet to indicate the type of weather outside. Collect the Sheets each day to pass out the next day or the next time your children meet.
3. At the end of four days, ask children to use their weather charts to talk about the weather for that period. Ask questions such as: *"Was it mostly sunny? Cloudy? Did a rainy day follow a cloudy day?"*

Challenge:
- Have children discuss different clothing they wear according to the weather. Mention different textures of clothing for different types of weather—wool, vinyl, cotton. Have children dress dolls for different types of weather.

Making Connections:
- Make a rain gauge from a straight-sided empty jar (pickle jar, jam jar): mark measurements (one quarter inches and one inch) with colored nail polish on the side of the jar; use wire to attach a gauge to a fence or pole outdoors. Have children observe and keep track of rain for a week or longer. (Science)

Books to Read:
Rain or Shine by Ronald Heuninck (Floris)
What will the Weather be Like Today by Paul Rogers (Greenwillow)

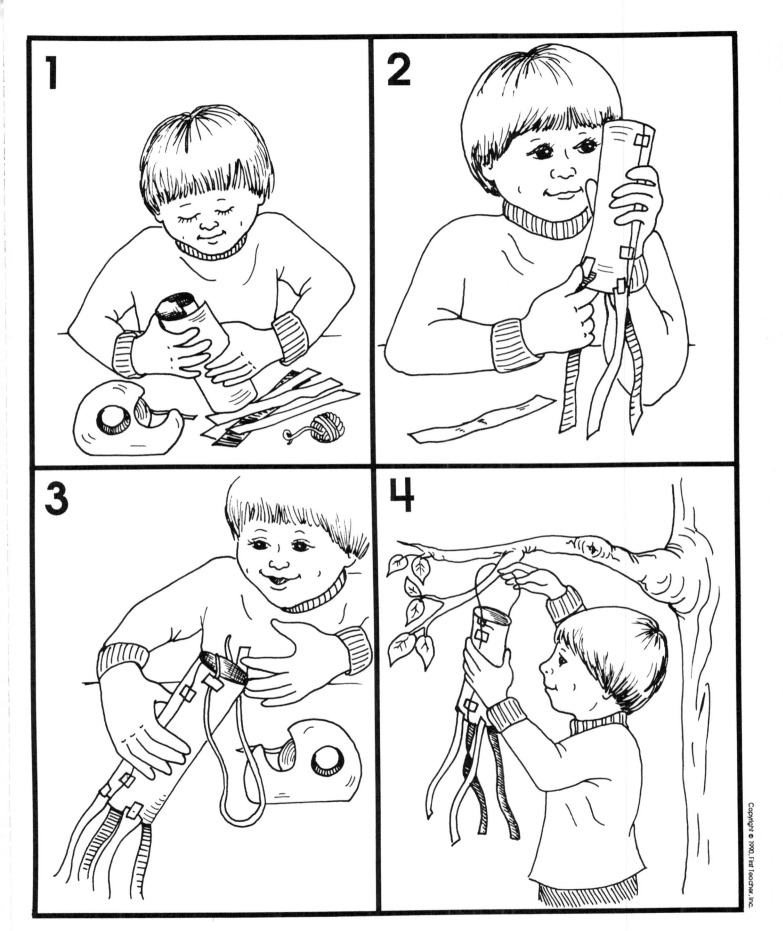

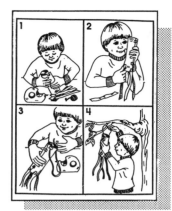

WIND SOCK

OBJECTIVES:
- to reinforce concept of sequence and following directions in sequence;
- to introduce and reinforce concept of basic North, South, East, West directions.

Wind and its changing force and direction become a reality for children in this colorful activity. It can be repeated at various times during the school year.

What You'll Need:
Copies of Activity 10 • blank pieces of paper • strips of colored tissue paper • yarn • tape.

Introduction:
Ask children questions which will tell you what they know about wind. *"Can we see wind? Can we feel the wind? Can we hear the wind? How can wind help us?"* Show a picture of a sailboat. Discuss how wind helps the sailor, how the sailor needs to know how fast and from which direction the wind is blowing. Tell children they will make a wind sock that will show from which direction the wind is blowing, and how hard or gently it is blowing.

What to Do:
1. Provide each child with a copy of Activity 10. Explain that they must follow the pictured directions carefully to make their own wind sock.
2. Demonstrate and then have children make a cylinder with a piece of paper, attaching the two ends with tape. Then help them follow the directions numbered 2, 3, and 4 to make their wind sock and attach the streamers.
3. Take the wind socks outdoors to let children observe how the wind makes the streamers move. Ask questions such as: *"Is the wind blowing today? Is it blowing hard or gently? How can you tell?"*

Challenges:
- Indicate North, South, East, and West for the children in your outdoor play area. Have children hold up their wind sock and name the direction from which the wind is blowing.
- Have children use copies of Activity 9 and record the number of windy days during a four day period.

Making Connections:
- Have children pretend they are a tree with moving branches. Ask: *"How would you move if the wind was blowing gently? How would you look if the wind was blowing hard on a blustery day?"* (Creative Movement)

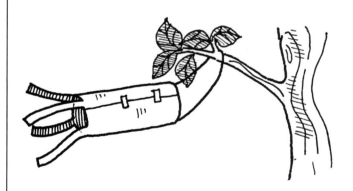

Books to Read:
Gilberto and the Wind by Marie Hall Ets (Viking)
Wind Blew by Pat Hutchins (Macmillan)

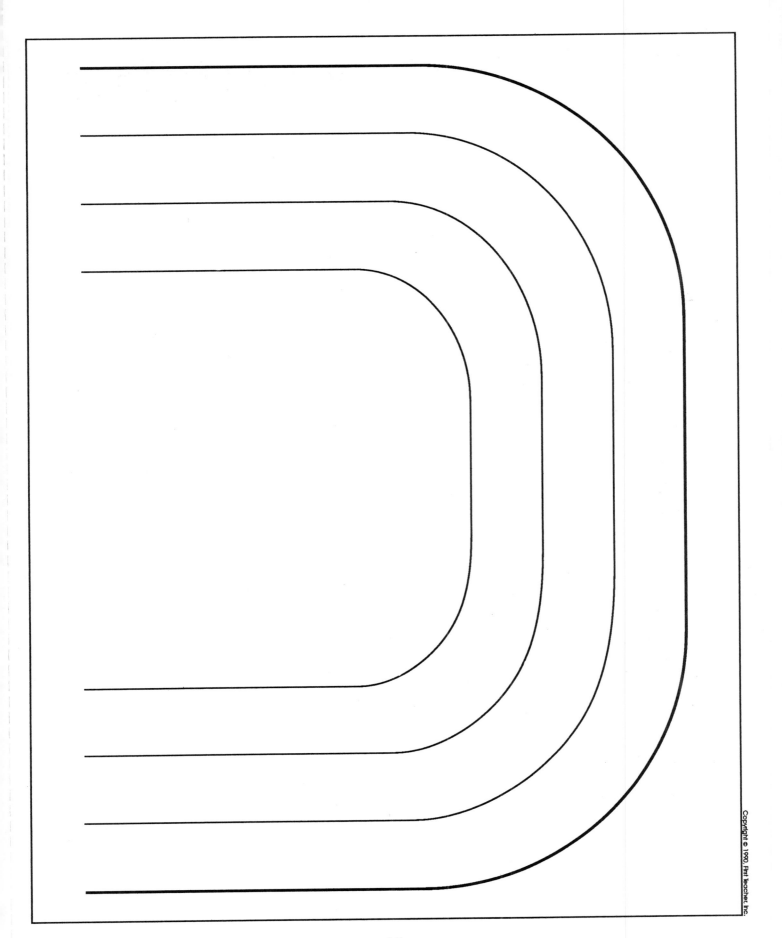

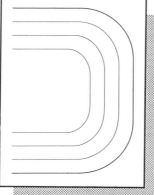

RAINBOWS

OBJECTIVES:

- to identify specific colors of a rainbow;
- to note details (colors);
- to reinforce concept of cause/effect.

A rainbow is the colorful result of the sun shining through drops of water. Children will love creating their own rainbows where colors blend just as they do in the sky.

What You'll Need:

Copies of Activity 11 • picture of a rainbow • wide water color paint brushes • tins of red, yellow, and blue water colors • sponges.

Introduction:

Discuss rainbows. Ask children: *"Who has seen a rainbow? Where do you see rainbows? When do we see a rainbow?"* Explain briefly what causes a rainbow. Then teach them the following song:

RAINBOWS (Tune: "Twinkle, Twinkle, Little Star")
Rainbow colors in the sky,
Looking at us from up high.
Purple, blue, a shade of green,
Yellow, orange and red are seen.
Rainbow colors in the sky,
Looking at us from up high.

Find a picture of a rainbow and have a child point to colors as everyone sings the song.

What to Do:

1. Provide each child with a copy of Activity 11 and a paintbrush. Have water color paints available for small groups to share.
2. Help children dampen the Activity Sheet thoroughly with a sponge.
3. Have children paint the top stripe on their Sheet with red water colors; have them paint the next stripe yellow, and the last stripe, blue. Have them paint a strip of red under the last stripe to create the color violet on their rainbows.
4. Ask children to tell you what colors they used. Then have children tell you what happened to the colors in their rainbows. What new colors do they see? Which colors blended?

Challenges:

- Have children choose a rainbow color and name objects they know of that color.
- Using another copy of the Activity Sheet (dry), have children glue rainbow colored yarn strips to the rainbow, in sequence, from top to bottom.

Making Connections:

- Talk about the pot of gold that Irish folklore says is at the end of the rainbow. (Social Studies, Language)
- Take children outdoors and create a rainbow by standing in the sun and spraying a fine spray from a hose. A rainbow will appear in spray. (Science)

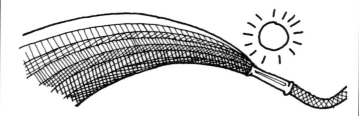

Books to Read:

A Rainbow of My Own by Don Freeman (Penguin)

THE FOUR SEASONS

OBJECTIVES:

- to identify the four seasons;
- to show sequence (of seasons);
- to classify (items appropriate for different seasons);
- to reinforce concept of cause/effect.

Changes of seasons bring changes of clothes, activities, and environment in the lives of children. Remember that children's responses to this activity will depend on where they live and on their personal experiences.

What You'll Need:

Copies of Activity 12 • scissors • paper plates • crayons or markers • glue.

Introduction:

Ask children questions about their knowledge of the different seasons: *"Who can name the seasons? What can you do only in the winter? Spring? Summer? Fall?"*

What to Do:

1. Provide each child with a copy of Activity 12. Have paper plates, crayons or markers, scissors, and glue available.
2. Help children identify the pictures on the Activity Sheet.
3. Have children name the current season. Then on the Sheet, have them find a picture they associate with that season and color it.
4. Help children identify the season that will come next and have them find a picture they associate with that season. Then have children color that picture. Continue with the last two seasons.
5. Give each child a paper plate that has been divided into quarters. Have children cut out the pictures on their Sheets. Demonstrate how to glue the picture for the current season in the top right hand section. Then have children glue the pic-

ture representing the next season in the section below. Continue pasting appropriate pictures for the remaining seasons clockwise around the plate.

Challenges:

- Have children cut out from magazines objects and articles of clothing they associate with each of the four seasons and glue them onto their paper plate. If pictures are too large for the space, help children tape them to the edge of the plate at the correct "season" section.
- Demonstrate and then help children make their plates into a seasonal clock by attaching a cardboard arrow to the center of the paper plate with a paper fastener. Hold up pictures taken or painted at different seasons and let children move the arrow to the appropriate season.

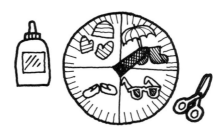

Making Connections:

- Play portions of the music *The Four Seasons* by Vivaldi. Have children draw pictures about what the music suggests. (Music, Art)

Books to Read:

Seasons by Suzanne Green (Doubleday)
Over and Over by Charlotte Zolotow (Harper and Row)

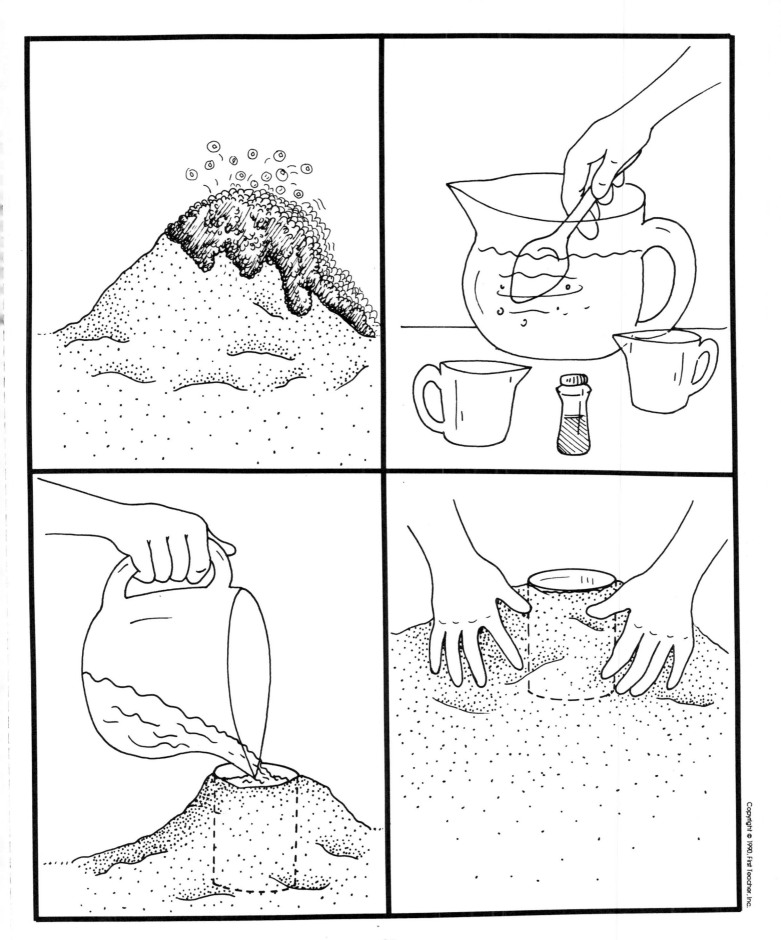

MAKE A VOLCANO

OBJECTIVES:

- to introduce and reinforce the concept of a volcano (formation, action, result);
- to show sequence (volcano experiment).

A simulated volcanic eruption provides an excellent way for children to experience scientific processes in action.

What You'll Need:

Copies of Activity 13 • measuring cups and spoons • water • red food coloring • a small can or jar • baking soda • dishwashing liquid • vinegar • scissors • glue • photographs of volcanos • pieces of blank paper.

Introduction:

Discuss volcanos, showing pictures and diagrams, if possible. An active volcano is an opening in the earth's surface around which a mountain of rock has built up. Hot gases and rocks shoot up through this hole at intervals. Introduce vocabulary such as *lava, erupt.* Using a map, show children where volcanos in North America are located (Mexico, Washington State).

What to Do:

1. With children helping to measure and pour, mix one-half cup of water, several drops of red food coloring, one-quarter cup of dishwashing liquid, and one-quarter cup of vinegar into a pitcher or clean bottle.
2. Add one-quarter cup of baking soda to a small, clean, and empty can or jar. Take the children, the can, and the pitcher of liquid you prepared and go outside. Bury the can in an outdoor sandbox or dirt pile; be sure the lip of the can or jar is sticking out of the sand.
3. Pour a little of the mixture from the pitcher into the can and watch it bubble up and over—just like lava from a volcano. Tell children that the baking soda mixes with

the vinegar and makes a gas called carbon dioxide that acts like the bubbles in a soda. In a real volcano, there is gas which causes liquid rock to bubble in the same way.

4. Return to the classroom and provide each child with a copy of Activity 13 and scissors. Make available glue and blank paper for small groups. Have children cut out the pictures on the Sheet and glue them in order on the paper to show how the class volcano was created.
5. Let children take turns describing the experiment and the result, using their pictures as a guide.

Challenge:

- Observe other mountain formations in pictures or outdoors; discuss their shape and size compared to volcanos.

Making Connections:

- Discuss the causes and actions of earthquakes and their similarities to volcanos (activity deep inside the earth, affecting the earth's surface). (Science)
- Play the first part of Igor Stravinsky's *Rite of Spring* (available on cassette) and encourage children to pretend they are volcanos or earthquakes as they move to the music. (Music, Creative Movement)

Book to Read:

What is a Volcano? by Chris Arvetis (Macmillan)

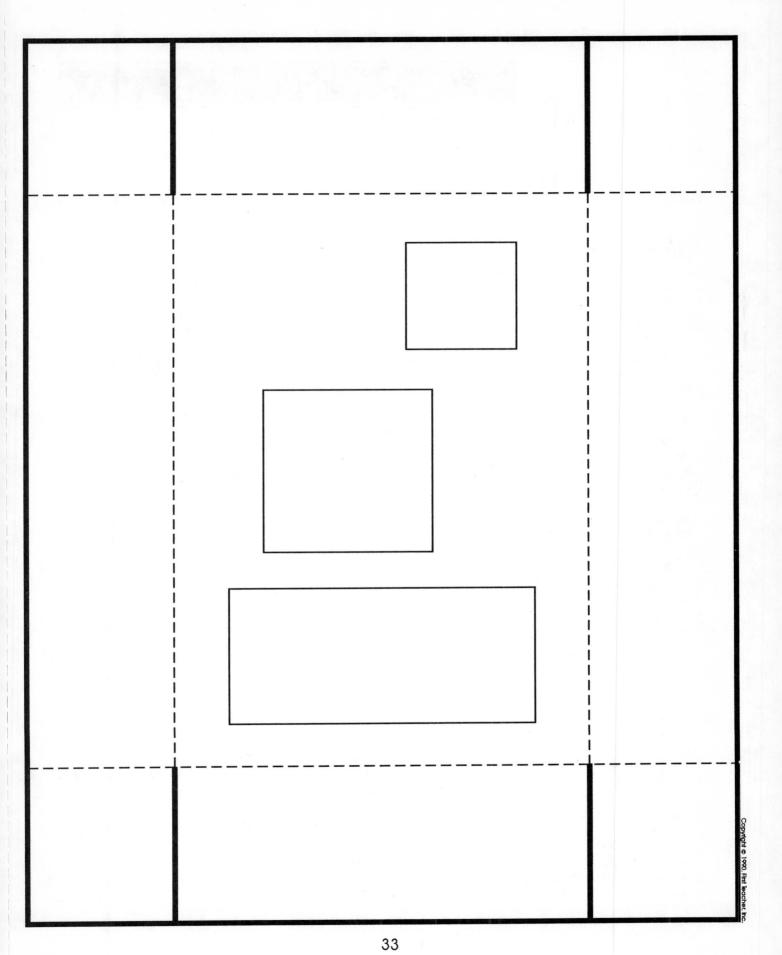

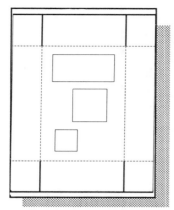

ROCK COLLECTION

OBJECTIVES:
- to reinforce observation skills;
- to order   (according to size);
- to classify (according to shape, size, texture).

Rocks are one of our planet's basic foundations. There are many kinds of rocks formed in many different ways, resulting in different colors and textures.

What You'll Need:
Copies of Activity 14 • scissors • tape • paper bags or small boxes.

Introduction:
Show children a variety of rocks or stones. Use terms such as *metamorphic, sedimentary, igneous.* Explain their meanings in simple words (metamorphic-made by changing from one form to another; sedimentary-made by pressing different layers of material together; igneous-made by first melting under great heat and then cooling). Those children who enjoy vocabulary will learn and understand these terms easily. Ask children to tell you about things they know that are made from rocks: for example, sidewalk, stone wall, fireplace, chimney, goldfish pond. If possible, find pictures that show layers of rocks. Talk about sand being tiny rocks. Tell children they will collect rocks and look at them carefully to note size, shape, color, and texture.

What to Do:
1. Provide each child with a copy of Activity 14, scissors, and tape. Explain that children are going to create trays to display rocks that they collect and study. Demonstrate and then help children make a tray out of the Activity Sheet by cutting on the lines at the four corners, folding up the sides, and attaching with

tape. Make sure the shapes are on the inside of the tray.

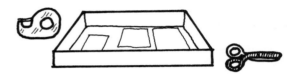

2. Talk about the shapes on the trays. Tell children that they will collect rocks outdoors and will choose the three most interesting ones to put in their tray.
3. Give each child a box or paper bag for collecting rocks. Then take a walk around the school and let children make their collections.
4. In the classroom, have children wash their rocks and then place three rocks on their display trays according to color, size, texture (rough, smooth), or shape.

Challenge:
- Help children prepare a chart that shows how many rocks they found together as a group; discuss appropriate headings for the chart and choose several. For example, Color: gray, white, brown—and the number for each color.

Making Connections:
- Play "On the Trail" from *Grand Canyon Suite* by Ferde Grofe. The composer uses instruments to depict donkey hooves on the rocky trail as they descend into the canyon. (Music)

Book to Read:
Sylvester and the Magic Pebble by William Steig (Simon and Schuster)

SUMMER FUN

OBJECTIVES:

- to identify items associated with the beach, water, and the sky;
- to classify (items belonging on land, in water, or in the sky).

Nothing points up the differences between earth, sea, and sky as well as a trip to the seashore or to a lake. Try to use this activity as a follow up to a field trip or when summer is fresh in children's minds.

What You'll Need:

Copies of Activity 15 • scissors • light blue paper • crayons or markers • cotton batting • sand • glue.

Introduction:

Talk with children about the fun they have during the summer. Note all the different places families go and all the different activities available for people to enjoy, either at home or away. Encourage children to suggest one or two things they might do or see at the seashore or at a lake.

What to Do:

1. Give each child a piece of blue paper.
2. Hold the paper horizontally. Demonstrate, then help chidren fold the bottom and top thirds of the paper toward the center of the paper. When the paper is opened, there will be three equal horizontal sections. Tell children they are going to make a beach scene.
3. Let children dot the bottom third of the paper with glue and sprinkle sand over it. Have them draw wavy lines across the middle third. Then have them glue wisps of cotton (for clouds) across the top to create a multi-sensory effect. Talk about the scene they have created.

4. Give each child a copy of Activity 15. Discuss the pictures. Ask children where they might see these items. Accept all reasonable answers.
5. Ask children to cut out the items and glue them where they belong on the beach scene: on the beach, in the water, or in the sky. Encourage them to explain their choices of places.

Challenge:

- Have children draw themselves in the picture. Have them glue a string from the kite to themselves. Then have children add one more object to each of the other two sections of the picture. Encourage them to tell classmates what they have added.

Making Connections:

- When children sing "Row, Row, Row Your Boat," have them sit on the floor facing a partner and row in time to music. Have them listen to music and row quickly when the music speeds up and row slowly when the music slows down. (Creative Movement, Music)

Book to Read:

Just Grandma and Me by Mercer Mayer (Golden)

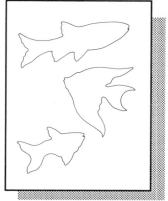

A HOME FOR THE FISH

OBJECTIVES:
- to classify (fish);
- to draw inferences (about environments for fish).

Fish live in many environments—the salty ocean, fresh water lakes, ponds, and in an aquarium in our home or classroom. Help children understand what fish need in order to live.

What You'll Need:
Copies of Activity 16 • crayons • watercolors • paintbrushes • water • pictures of fish.

Introduction:

Teach children the following poem:

LITTLE FISH

Little fish, little fish, swimming in the bay,
Little fish, little fish, please come here and play.
Little fish, little fish, swimming in the sea,
Little fish, little fish, tell me what you see.
Little fish, little fish, swimming in the brook,
Little fish, little fish, watch out for a hook!
Little fish, little fish, in the bowl so round,
Little fish, little fish, you are safe and sound!

If possible, have a goldfish in a bowl for children to observe and adopt as a classroom pet. Show pictures of and talk about fish environments—fresh and salt water, and plants. Introduce the term *aquarium*. Talk about different types of fish—those that we eat and those that are on display in an aquarium.

What to Do:
1. Provide each child with a copy of Activity 16. Have crayons, paper, and glue available.
2. Help children identify the pictures on the Activity Sheet as outlines of fish. Have children use crayons or markers to color the fish.
3. Tell children that they are going to create a home—an environment—for their fish. Let children decide whether their fish are going to live in the ocean or in an aquarium. Have them draw and color other details—plants, other fish, shells, and so on.
4. Ask children what is missing from their pictures that all fish would need to live. Give children watercolors and paintbrushes and have them paint over the entire paper with light blue or light green paint to create a watery effect.

Challenge:
- Have children cover their picture with light blue cellophane to further create the effect of water.

Making Connections:
- If possible, visit your local aquarium. Have children write a story and draw pictures about what they see. (Language)
- Play "The Aquarium" from *Carnival of Animals* by Camille Saint-Saens. Help children notice sounds that represent bubbles and the flowing rhythm that suggests swimming. (Music)

Book to Read:
I am a Fisherman by D. Swayne (Harper)

THINGS IN THE SKY

OBJECTIVES:
- to identify specific objects observed in the sky;
- to classify (objects seen in the sky).

We see many different things when we look at the sky. Some things we see at night, others by day. Some objects are a part of nature, others are put there by people.

What You'll Need:
Copies of Activity 17 • crayons or markers • scissors • glue • light blue and black pieces of paper • pictures of flying animals and insects, planes, rockets and other people-made flying objects.

Introduction:
Ask children to close their eyes and pretend they are looking at the sky. Ask questions such as: *"What could you see during the day? What would you see at night?"* Talk about things we see in the sky that are a part of nature such as birds, bats, clouds, rainbows, butterflies, stars, sun, moon, and things that are made by people such as kites, balloons, airplanes, helicopters, blimps, rockets. Show children pictures of examples, if possible.

What to Do:
1. Provide children with copies of Activity 17. Have crayons or markers, stars and stickers, scissors, colored paper, and glue available.
2. Help children identify the pictures on the Activity Sheet. Have children color and cut out each picture.
3. Help children sort objects according to the categories: natural and people-made.
4. Have children choose colored paper to represent either the daytime or nighttime sky. Have them choose the items they think they would see in the sky at that time of day.

5. Have children glue the pictures they chose onto the appropriate piece of paper. Remind children that some of the items, like the moon, may be visible in both the day and night sky, so many combinations are possible. Have children tell you about their pictures and why they chose the items they did to put in the sky.

Challenge:
- Have children choose one of the objects in the sky—natural or made by people—and tell what they would see and do if they were up in the sky with or in that object.

Making Connections:
- Take a walk and have children look at shapes of the cloud formations. Ask them to tell you what they imagine these shapes to be. Return to class. Have children make a cloud collage by gluing cotton balls in various configurations on blue paper. (Art)

Books to Read:
Harold's Trip to the Sky by Crockett Johnson (Harper and Row)
The Gooney War by Wendy Pfeffer (Betterway)

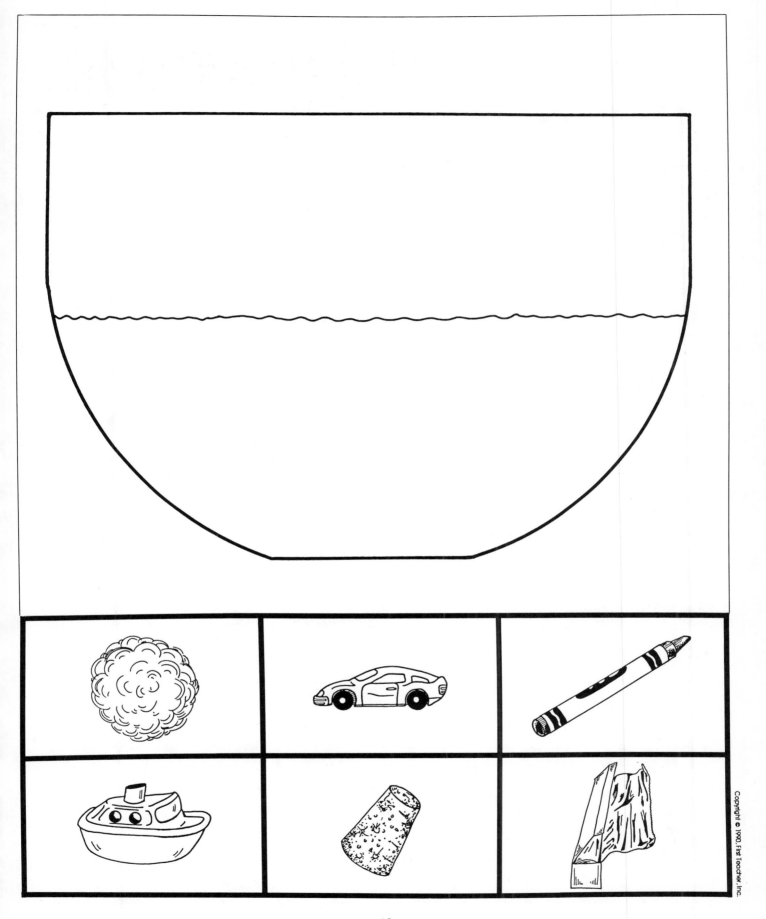

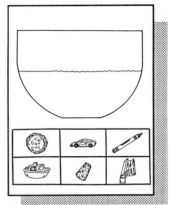

SINK AND FLOAT

OBJECTIVES:
- to introduce the concepts of floating and sinking;
- to note details (in an experiment);
- to classify (objects that sink and float).

Some objects in our environment sink in water, whereas others float. Help children to observe and experiment with various objects to discover what sinks and what floats. This activity is best done in small groups so that everyone may have a chance try it.

What You'll Need:
Copies of Activity 18 • bowl of water • tin foil • crayons (without paper wrapping) • corks • cotton balls • metal toy car • plastic toy boat • scissors • glue.

Introduction:
Ask children if they know what it means to float. Relate this concept to swimming and bathing in a bathtub. Talk about why some objects float and some do not. When an object goes to the bottom of the water, we say it sinks. Talk about the term *experiment*. Help children understand that when they try things out to see if their ideas are correct, they are experimenting. Tell children that they are going to be doing an experiment to see which things float in water and which things sink.

What to Do:
1. Provide each child with a copy of Activity 18. Have scissors and glue available.
2. Help children identify the objects pictured on the Activity Sheet. Talk about what the objects are probably made of. Tell children that on their Sheet they will record the results of their experiment.
3. Now show children a bowl of water and real examples of the objects pictured on the Sheet. Make sure there are enough real objects for each child to be able to do the experiment by herself. Tell children that they are to place each type of object in the bowl to determine which ones float on top of the water and which ones sink to the bottom of the bowl. Have them predict what will happen to each object before putting it in water.

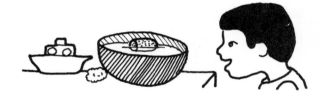

4. After they have determined whether an object sinks or floats, have children cut out the picture of that object on the Sheet and glue it either on top of the water line on the bowl or at the bottom of the bowl.

Challenge:
- Have children count how many objects in the experiment floated and how many sank. Brainstorm with children why certain objects sank and others floated.

Making Connections:
- Continue to experiment with the sink and float phenomenon. Keep a running list of "sinkers" and "floaters" as children test more and more items. (Science)

Book to Read:
What Floats? by Mary Brewer (Children's Press)

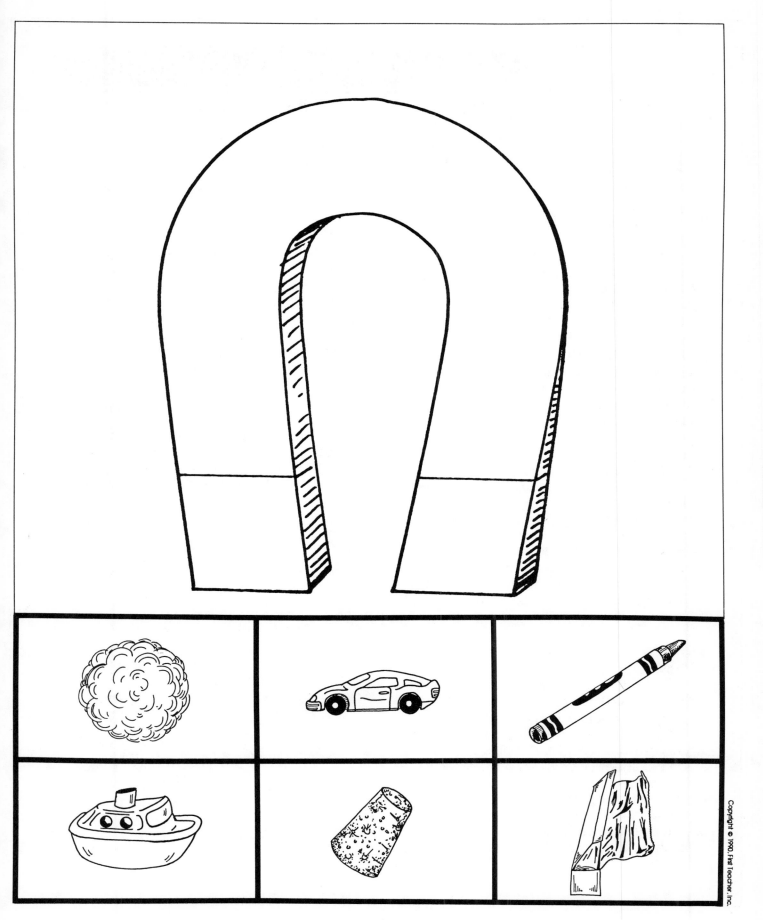

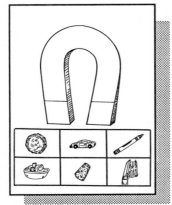

MAGNET FUN

OBJECTIVES:
- to discover the properties of a magnet;
- to note details (in an experiment);
- to classify (objects attracted to and repelled by a magnet).

Young children enjoy playing with magnets of all sizes and shapes. They often think that magnets work by magic. Help children do a simple experiment that will encourage them to study these fascinating objects further.

What You'll Need:
Copies of Activity 19 • scissors • glue •cotton balls • tin foil • crayons • plastic boats • metal toy cars •cork • bar magnets or horseshoe magnets.

Introduction:
Show a magnet to children to see if they can identify it. Discuss how certain objects will stick to magnets and others will not. (To be attracted to the magnet, objects must contain a certain metal.) Demonstrate the magnet's capabilities with classroom objects. Review the term *experiment*. Tell children that they are going to do some experiments to see which objects stick to a magnet and which do not.

What to Do:
1. Provide each child with a copy of Activity 19. Have scissors and glue available. Have several sets of the objects pictured on the Activity Sheet and several magnets also available.
2. Help children identify the objects pictured on the Sheet. If possible, have at least one horseshoe magnet for children to see, if they are going to use bar magnets for their experiments.
3. Have children experiment with real examples of the objects pictured on the

Sheet to see if they stick to a magnet or not.
4. Have children cut out the pictures of objects on the Sheet. Then have children glue the pictures that represent objects that stuck to the magnet on the picture of the magnet as a record of the results of the actual experiments.

Challenge:
- Have children explore the classroom looking for other objects to experiment with and discover which ones will be attracted to the magnet. Make a class chart to list objects attracted to the magnet and those not attracted.

Making Connections:
- Have children use markers, yarn, glitter, etc. to decorate small precut circles of oaktag. Glue these onto small magnets and use on refrigerators to hold notes. (Art)
- Have children place a paper clip under a small piece of paper and then under a piece of cloth. Have them guess what will happen each time. (Magnet will pick up paper clip through both paper and cloth.) (Science)

Book to Read:
Micky's Magnet by Franklin Branley (Scholastic)

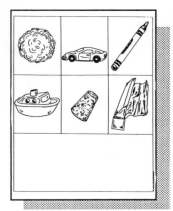

ABSORPTION

OBJECTIVES:
- to introduce the concept of absorption;
- to note details (in an experiment);
- to classify (objects that absorb water and those that do not).

Help children experiment with objects and water to determine which materials absorb water and which do not.

What You'll Need:
Copies of Activity 20 • vinyl raincoat • watercolors • paintbrushes • medicine droppers • small dishes of water • cotton balls • plastic boats • metal toy cars • corks • tin foil • crayons.

Introduction:
Show children a slicker-type raincoat. Talk about the material from which it is made—vinyl. Ask children what they think will happen to water on the vinyl. Show them that water runs off the material—it does not sink into the material or become absorbed.. Then say to children: *"Today we will do an experiment to find out what materials will absorb water and what will not."*

What to Do:
1. Provide each child with a copy of Activity 20. Have water colors and brushes available. Have the materials pictured on the Activity Sheet, medicine droppers, and dishes of water ready for children to use.
2. Help children identify the objects on the Sheet. Help children fill a medicine dropper with water (review, if necessary), and place a drop on each object. Have them observe to see whether or not the drop is absorbed.
3. To record their results, have children use blue watercolor to paint over those objects (on the Sheet) which absorbed water.

4. Have children experiment with other objects and materials. Help children draw one object that absorbs water in the empty box at the bottom of the Activity Sheet and paint it with watercolor.

Challenge:
- Have children count the number of objects that absorbed water and the ones that did not. Help children make a class chart to record their findings.

Making Connections:
- Trim the ends off of a stalk of celery or trim the stem of a carnation. Place the celery or carnation in a glass of water with food coloring added. Ask children to note what happens. (Flower or stalk will turn the color of the water; colored water is absorbed into the stalk or flower.) (Science)

- Let children add water to a dry sponge. Ask them to tell what happens.

Book to Read:
Water is Wet by Penny Pollock (Putnam)

HOT OR COLD

OBJECTIVES:

- to compare (hot and cold);
- to experiment and note details;
- to reinforce the concept of absorption (heat)

The sun produces heat that makes us warm and helps plants and trees grow. Help children do this experiment to see what types of objects absorb the heat from the sun the fastest.

What You'll Need:

Copies of Activity 21 • tin foil • plastic toy boat • cotton ball • metal toy car • cork • red and yellow crayons or markers.

Introduction:

Choose a warm, very sunny day. Talk about the sun. Ask questions such as: *How do you know the sun is out there? Can you feel it? Can you touch it? How do you feel when the sun is shining directly on you? Does it touch you?* Show pictures of the sun. Give children an explanation like the following: *The sun is very, very hot. It is a giant ball of fire. Heat comes out from the sun and certain types of objects absorb it, just as certain types of objects absorb water (see Activity 20). When objects absorb the heat from the sun, they become hot themselves.*

Review the term *experiment*. Propose to children that they do an experiment to discover what types of objects absorb the sun's heat.

What to Do:

1. Provide each child with a copy of Activity 21. Have red and yellow crayons or markers available.
2. Help children identify the objects on the Activity Sheet, including the sun. Have them color the sun and its rays red and yellow.
3. Have children help you place outside in the sunshine or on a window ledge a real example of each object pictured on the Sheet.
4. Before children go home <u>and</u> before the sun moves, let them touch each object to see if it is warm from the sun.
5. Have children record the results of their experiment. If the real objects pictured on their Sheet felt warm, having absorbed the heat of the sun, have children color those objects on their Sheet.

Challenge:

- Place two pieces of paper in the sun— one black and the other one white. Keep track of the time it takes for each piece of paper to get warm. Talk about the results.

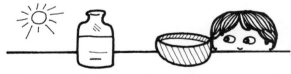

Making Connections:

- If you have completed Activities 18, 19, and 20, review the results and talk about characteristics of the various objects used in the experiments. For example, plastic boats float, don't absorb water, and don't get hot in the sun. Metal cars are attracted to magnets and they also get hot in the sun. Make a chart to show the characteristics of the six objects used in the experiments.

Book to Read:

Shine, Sun by Carol Greene (Children's Press)